Edwin

A play

John Mortimer

Samuel French—London
New York-Toronto-Hollywood

30130 071817802

ISBN 0 573 12101 X

Please see page iv for further copyright information

EDWIN

First broadcast by BBC Radio on 16 October 1982 as one of its 60th Anniversary Plays, with the following cast:

Sir Fennimore Truscott	Emlyn Williams
Lady Margaret Truscott	Sylvia Coleridge
Tom Marjoriebanks	Michael Gough

Later the play was produced by Anglia Television with the following cast:

Sir Fennimore Truscott	Alec Guinness
Lady Margaret Truscott	Renée Asherson
Tom Marjoriebanks	Paul Rogers

In this stage version of the play, two male extras are required

The action takes place in the garden of the Truscotts' house, Gallows Corner, in Suffolk

Time – A summer's day in the present

Scene 1	Before lunch
Scene 2	After lunch

EDWIN

Scene 1

The large, moderately well-kept garden of a large Victorian house in the Suffolk countryside. Summer. Lunchtime

There is a mulberry tree on the lawn under which are four basket chairs, one of which we never see used throughout the play. There is also a garden table. Across the lawn we can see an old, ornate conservatory built on to the house, its door half-open. The conservatory glass is green with moss and algae and is opaque, but we can see the shapes of people as they pass through it on their way from the house to the garden

As the Curtain *rises, Sir Fennimore Truscott, a retired Judge, is sitting in one of the chairs, dozing. He is in old tweeds, with a panama hat on the ground beside him. He talks to himself as though he is summing up in one of his old cases*

Truscott (*to himself*) I put it to you, Marshbanks, you rogered my wife. The charge is that you, Thomas *Marjorie*banks, feloniously and unlawfully did roger Lady Margaret Truscott. What day, exactly, what squalid night, or what furtive afternoon? Or was it immediately after breakfast when I had caught the eight-fifteen up to Temple Station and the Law Courts? Did you dive in here, Marjorie, and take her warm in her housecoat while she was watering in the conservatory? What was your excuse for invading my property? Half a dozen eggs? I remember the nasty habit you had of keeping fowl! That was your war work, wasn't it? Boiling kitchen scraps for a run of bedraggled and malicious birds. Thomas Marjoriebanks, V.C. Violated chickens! A man not to be trusted with anything warm and feathered. What sort of sentence would that carry, I wonder? Unlawful intercourse with the wife of a High Court Judge, a Red Judge, a Judge of the utmost seniority, what sort of sentence would that attract?

Margaret appears in the conservatory doorway. She is Truscott's age but shows every sign of having once been beautiful

Margaret (*calling*) Fen!

Truscott (*to himself*) Death is the least sentence I could pass, having given due weight to all mitigating circumstances.

Margaret (*coming out of the conservatory and closing the door behind her*) What're you doing?

Truscott Arriving at some sort of judgement.

Margaret Sitting under the old mulberry tree and dozing, that's what you've been doing. You'll have to bestir yourself soon.

Truscott I'm perfectly capable of bestirring myself, thank you.

Margaret Edwin'll be here directly. Your son will be here before very long. We're going to lay on a decent spread for Edwin. Have you seen to the wine?

Truscott Of course I've seen to the wine. Half a dozen bottles up from the cellar. It's been waiting there for Edwin for most of his life. Patience has made the claret ... something quite remarkable, I fancy ...

There is a pause, during which Margaret moves away and looks around the garden

Margaret The colchicums are all out. The autumn crocus.

Truscott What?

Margaret The autumn crocus, Fen. The naked ladies.

Truscott Naked ladies! Who calls them that?

Margaret Tom does. Tom always calls them "naked ladies."

Truscott (*with contempt*) Tom would. Tom Marjoriebanks! It all adds up.

Margaret Adds up to what?

Truscott Small pieces of evidence, all circumstantial. Taken as a whole they provide a pretty formidable case.

Margaret No need to think of cases now you've retired, dear.

Truscott You think I can shrug off the responsibility of judgement with the scarlet and ermine? I'm sitting here in mufti, I know. Under the mulberry. But I still have to reach a *decision*.

Margaret We'll soon be having to take in the geraniums.

Truscott What have the geraniums got to do with it?

Margaret The weather's bright enough now, but it's deceptive. I'll soon be taking them in to the conservatory.

Truscott Why on earth?

Margaret To save them being nipped by an early frost.

Truscott Don't mollycoddle them! Anyway, isn't that a job for Cattermole?

Margaret Cattermole's got his work cut out; he's weeding the cabbages. Anyway, Cattermole's not as young as he used to be.

Truscott Don't keep a dog and bark yourself.

Margaret The hibiscus came too late! Our soil's not rich enough.

Truscott We keep Cattermole as a jobbing gardener and you choose to pot your own geraniums. Why can't they stand out in the frost and be nipped like the rest of humanity?

Margaret Because they're not at all like the rest of humanity!

Truscott Oh, really? What's so different about them, then?

Margaret (*moving towards the conservatory*) They're geraniums.

Truscott Where are you going?

Margaret Just time to water things before I get the lunch laid.

Truscott Don't go!

Margaret Only into the conservatory.

Truscott Isn't that rather asking for trouble?

Margaret (*reaching the door*) What did you say?

Truscott Typical of a woman. They do rather ask for trouble ...

Margaret (*opening the conservatory door*) What did you say, Fennimore?

Truscott Nothing. I said absolutely nothing.

Margaret exits into the conservatory

(*To himself*) Members of the Jury. We now come to the details
of this rather sordid story, one that will be painful to you, I have
no doubt. It is some considerable time ago now that Lady
Margaret Truscott, a woman a good deal younger than she is
today, took the unwise step of going, alone and unprotected,
into her husband's conservatory for the perfectly proper pur-
pose of watering pot plants. Members of the Jury, you will see
that there are two entrances to the conservatory, one leading out
to the garden, the other into the hall of the matrimonial home,
Gallows Corner near Drackham in the County of Suffolk. The
view from outside is somewhat obscured by the greenish haze
and deposit of algae upon the glass, and by the extensive fronds
of those pampered plants which are apparently too delicate to
rough it down the border with the hardy perennials. This makes
the conservatory an ideal place for private illegality. An intent
observer seated beneath the old mulberry tree on the lawn
might have seen, however, through the greenish mist, a second
figure invade the glasshouse from the hall entrance and position itself unnaturally close to Lady Truscott. Unfortunately
you, Members of the Jury, were not seated beneath that tree on
that particular morning. Had you been I do not think you would
have been in any doubt as to the marauder's identity. Quite
clearly it was none other than the accused, the man Thomas
Marjoriebanks. (*He shuts his eyes*)

*The conservatory door opens and Margaret comes out with
Tom Marjoriebanks, a man of the same age, who is dressed in
a vaguely artistic fashion in a pink shirt, spotted bow tie, old
tweed jacket and flannel trousers. He is carrying a tray with a
decanter and four sherry glasses. Tom is whistling the tune of*

"Your Tiny Hand Is Frozen" from La Bohème. *They walk towards Truscott*

Margaret Wake up, Fen! Tom's here ... (*To Tom*) He's dozing again! Dozing under the mulberry tree. Put the sherry down there, Tom, why don't you.

Tom stops whistling and puts the tray down on the garden table. He looks at Truscott, who appears to be asleep. Tom and Margaret talk quietly, trying not to wake him up

Tom Time hangs heavy on his hands now, I expect. (*He pours two glasses of sherry*)

Margaret There's so little for a retired judge to do. He's lost without his trials. Of course, he still manages to try things whenever he can. Most of the week he's been trying Haversack for burying his bone in the rose bed.

Tom (*handing a glass of sherry to Margaret*) What was the verdict?

Margaret Not reached. (*She raises her glass to Tom and drinks*) Fen likes to drag these things out as long as possible. Oh, and he prepared an indictment against a wasp which kept landing on his toast and marmalade when we had breakfast out there.

Tom He'd try anything. (*He drinks*)

Truscott (*opening his eyes;loudly*) You're right, Marshbanks! Any kind of pest that exceeds its rights.

Margaret Surely a wasp has a right to the garden, Fennimore?

Truscott Every right includes a duty.

Tom (*pouring a third glass of sherry*) What's the duty of a wasp?

Truscott Not to dabble its feet in my bloody marmalade!

Margaret God created wasps, dear. They're entitled to settle. (*She sits in one of the chairs*)

Truscott That's a typical do-gooder's point of view. My wife's a Red, Marshbanks. I hope you appreciate that?

Tom (*handing the third sherry to Truscott*) It must be a hard life for you, Fennimore, without any real criminals.

Truscott Real criminals? Oh, I can find *plenty* of them! (*He looks at Tom and drinks*)

Margaret (*looking round the garden*) We're not usually here when the autumn crocus is out. We're usually in Dieppe, the three of us.

Truscott I don't like that hotel in Dieppe any more. Not since they put music in the lift.

Margaret We could always find another hotel.

Truscott Typical Red, my wife. She wants change all the time!

Tom I missed our holiday this year, all the same. (*He sits and drinks sherry*)

Truscott Can't say I missed seeing you fumble for your francs — in slow motion — every time *l'addition* was presented!

Tom What have you two been doing?

Margaret We were arguing about geraniums. Fen thinks I mollycoddle them.

Tom What do you favour for geraniums, Fennimore? Borstal training? The short, sharp shock ?

Truscott A little cold weather does no-one any harm. I say, Marshbanks, we've not asked you to luncheon, have we?

Tom Of course you have! Today's the great day, isn't it? The return of the prodigal. What did I smell coming through the house? Fatted calf?

Truscott (*suspicious*) Came through the house, did you?

Margaret Tom helped me to carry out the sherry.

Truscott Oh, and what else did he help you do? (*He empties his glass*)

Margaret Nothing else.

Tom Care for a refill, old fellow? (*He gets up and fetches the decanter*)

Truscott *Old*? I like that — "old" coming from you!

Tom (*refilling their glasses*) Here, Margaret ...

Margaret Thank you. We're all three old, Fen. No need to rub it in.

Truscott (*to himself*) "Consider my client's age, my Lord. Is he to die in prison?" Why is your client so particular — about where he dies?

Tom (*putting down the decanter and raising his glass*) Well. Here's to Edwin!

Truscott My boy, Edwin!

Tom Fatted calf for Edwin. That's what I smelled, coming through the house. (*He sits*)

Truscott Not fatted calf. A trifle of roast duck, apple sauce, a loganberry pie swimming in cream. He chose that for his last supper before going back to school one half, I remember. "Edwin," I said to the boy, "if you make such wise decisions throughout your life you will grow to be a great and good man ..."

Tom And has he, do you think?

Truscott Has he what?

Tom Grown to be a great and good man.

Truscott That remains to be seen.

Margaret If Edwin's happy, that's all we care about.

Truscott Margaret, being a bloody Red, I mean, would say that!

Tom Oh, I agree with Maggie!

Truscott Maggie ... ?

Tom Well, with Margaret. What have we to strive for but the greatest happiness of the greatest number?

Truscott (*with contempt*) The simple-minded creed of a fellow who makes crockery!

Margaret You really cannot describe Tom, whose glazed pottery is shown in *art galleries*, as "a fellow who makes crockery."

Truscott Crockery or pottery, I don't know what's the difference. Anyway, what's the use of your *artistic* pots, Marshbanks? Anyone ever served up a decent stew in one?

Tom Anyone ever served up a decent stew in one of your legal decisions?

Margaret Oh, well done, Tom! Awfully good shot ...

Truscott It wasn't well done at all! I hope you don't think the judicial function can be compared in any shape or form to spinning a bit of mud around and cooking it into a vague evocation of a peasant chamber pot which can usefully hold dead bullrushes in a Hampstead bed-sitter. Neither has the art of judgement any connection with hand weaving, macramé, *petit point* or the making of stamped leather covers for the telephone directory.

Tom At least no one gets sent to prison by a peasant chamber pot.

Truscott Exactly! Haven't you noticed, the tide's gone down in this sherry glass? Can I trouble you for another drop of my Amontillado?

Margaret Do the honours, Tom.

Tom gets up, refills their glasses

I should have liked Edwin to have followed an artistic career. At one time I thought he had a future with the pencil.

Truscott He has a far better future than that.

Tom In the world ... of business? (*He sits*)

Truscott Margaret can't stand "business". She was a pillar of the local Fabians at the time of my boy's birth. You bicycled with them, didn't you, Margaret?

Margaret Bicycling was over years ago. We used to go on rambles, though. And summer schools to Dartington Hall ...

Truscott A couple of those revolutionary rambles and she thought she'd give birth to Vladimir Ilyich Lenin! Lucky Edwin didn't take after his mother. He found all those Socialists in knickerbockers extremely embarrassing.

Margaret I have never seen anybody in knickerbockers! Never in my life.

Truscott My boy was always on the side of authority. Edwin was a monitor at his prep school.

Margaret I always felt Edwin was too sensitive to be a monitor.

Truscott A monitor at Boglands on the Norfolk coast. At "Boggers" he kept some sort of law and order, in an extremely primitive society. He was a firm but just man, at the age of ten, as I remember it.

Margaret He wasn't a monitor at his big school.

Truscott His "big" school? What's this language of the nursery? Lawnhurst. Founded by an Elizabethan clothier. Cold bathed through Victorian England as a harsh nursery for Archbishops and Governors of New South Wales. Edwin's "big" school. "Biggies"... "big jobs".

Margaret Edwin was never a monitor at Lawnhurst.

Truscott Was he not? I don't entirely remember.

Tom *I* remember.

Truscott What, Marshbanks? What do you remember ?

Tom I remember Edwin wrote to me from Lawnhurst. He said he'd joined the Madrigal Society.

Truscott (*appalled*) *Madrigal* Society?

Margaret He said he used to go brass-rubbing in the local churches. On a bicycle. It got him out of the football.

Truscott Brass-rubbing! He was having you on, Tom.

Tom He showed me his rubbings. And some of his water-colours were quite decorative. He'd hang them on the walls of his study.

Truscott I never saw any such thing.

Tom Perhaps he took them down when you came to visit, Fennimore.

Truscott All I saw in his study was a photograph of the football team.

Tom Put up, probably, just to please you.

Truscott Why did he write to *you*, anyway?

Tom What?

Truscott Why did he write letters to *you*, from Lawnhurst?

Tom As a sort of honorary uncle ...

Truscott A relation?

Tom Not really. A family friend.

Truscott Friend or relation?

Tom Just a friend.

Truscott No *blood* relation! (*He pauses*) It's wishful thinking,
Marshbanks. I don't believe Edwin wrote to you at all. (*He
pauses again*) You had no issue, did you?

Tom What?

Truscott No fruit of your loins. No part of you whatever, Tom,
to thrust forth into the future. You will die and there'll be
nothing left of you, except a few impractical china objects and
your old tweed jacket swinging on a coat hanger. That is until
they pack it up and give it to Oxfam.

Tom My dear Fennimore. Do *you* claim immortality?

Truscott Edwin will carry on a certain tradition. He is carrying
on ... certain standards! (*He pauses*) They're keeping him busy
out in Canada, apparently. Well, Edwin's not afraid of work.
Well, the boy's letters were always scrappy.

Tom Not at all.

Truscott What?

Tom I said not at all. His letters from school to me were always
long.

Truscott Long letters to *you*? Oh, yes, what about?

Tom About the leaves falling. About the wind. Breaking into
poetry sometimes.

Truscott You live in a world of fantasy! (*He pauses*) Any good?

Tom What?

Truscott Edwin's poetry.

Tom And clouds. I believe it was about clouds. That sort of
thing ...

Truscott No bloody good then, eh?

Margaret Don't you be so sure, Fen.

Truscott What?

Margaret Don't you be so sure it wasn't good. Edwin had a sensitive ear for verse.

Truscott A sensitive ear! I can't say I ever noticed.

Tom whistles the Bohème *aria, continuing under the following*

(*To himself*) You hear that whistle, Members of the Jury? It may be an important piece of the evidence. (*Aloud*) What are you whistling, Marshbanks, exactly?

Margaret He always whistles that.

Truscott He always what?

Margaret He whistled it, I remember, during air raids.

Truscott The war years ...

Margaret Such a happy time. The war years. The summers were so marvellous.

Truscott And you could have lunch at the Savoy and change left over from a ten-pound note.

Margaret And Tom kept chickens. Do you remember, Tom? You used to bring us eggs. (*She pauses*) Tom kept chickens — and I was pregnant with Edwin.

Truscott You were pregnant with our boy, and Tom used to come round whistling. (*To Tom*) You used to whistle like a grocer's boy, bringing round eggs. (*He pauses*) Edwin didn't write to you from Canada?

Tom No. No, in Canada Edwin became strangely silent.

Truscott Well, you know what boys are.

Margaret Boys?

Truscott When they get a bit of independence for the first time. When they go out to the colonies. Run wild for a few years. Get the edges knocked off them. Well, it's only to be expected.

Tom You think Edwin's been running wild?

Truscott Wouldn't surprise me in the least. I don't mean anything sinister. I don't mean anything seriously immoral.

But it wouldn't surprise me if he hadn't been ... well, log-cabinning ... out in the Rockies or somewhere.

Margaret His letters to me are all from Global Computers.

Truscott Computers? Oh, yes. Of course. Well, I expect that's just what he tells his mother. Log-cabinning, I dare say. Something of that nature. (*He pauses*) He's written to you, then?

Margaret Written occasionally. (*She stands up*)

Truscott You didn't tell me.

Margaret (*moving towards the conservatory and the house*) I'll go and look at the duck. See if the oven needs turning up.

Truscott (*calling after her*) Why didn't you show me the letters, madam?

Margaret exits into the conservatory; we see her shadowy figure disappear behind the glass

Tom She's gone, Fennimore. Maggie has gone into the house.

Truscott (*to himself*) Madam, I demand an answer to my question. The witness has clearly something to hide. You might think that a man, Members of the Jury, would be interested above all things in a letter from his son, his own flesh and blood. (*Pause*) That is, of course, if he is his own flesh and blood ...

Tom whistles

The presumption of legitimate birth is strong. Nothing is stronger.

Tom stops whistling and laughs

Tom She's marvellous ... old Maggie.

Truscott Marvellous! Is that your view of Margaret?

Tom I mean. She's a marvellous wife, your Margaret.

Truscott My Margaret ... (*He pauses*) Fancy her, don't you? (*To himself*) It is, of course, the vital question.

Tom Oh, enormously.

Truscott (*to himself*) Is the accused suffering from ridiculous over-confidence — or is the guilt so great that he sees no alternative to an admission?

Tom (*laughing*) Of course I fancy her. Always did. Since the first day you brought her here.

Truscott (*to himself*) Bringing her here. That was my mistake. To Gallows Corner. Where the next-door-neighbour was a lecherous potter. A fellow with nothing better to do than spin shit-coloured crocks for holding spills in front of gas fires in Welwyn Garden City and leer through conservatory windows at the other fellow's wife.

Tom I remember that first day you brought her here. After your old father died.

Truscott (*to himself*) The house was empty. We were picnicking in a dusty kitchen. "Gallows Corner" seemed an appropriate sort of name, I said, as I'd just been made up to a High Court Judge, a fellow who then had it in his power to order, in extreme cases of course, a good topping.

Tom She came over to borrow a little milk.

Truscott She was always forgetful.

Tom She wore a blue linen dress, as I remember it. No stockings, and plimsolls.

Truscott She dressed like a revolutionary. A Judge's wife, wearing plimsolls — like a bloody Communist!

Tom Her hair was tied back with a ribbon. That was what struck me so forcibly.

Truscott (*puzzled*) Red hair?

Tom Well, surely the colour of her hair is ...

Truscott Grey is what I would say about it. Entirely grey.

Tom But then — then it was red, surely?

Truscott I would have described it as auburn. And held back with a tortoiseshell comb. I thought she was a long time borrowing the milk.

Tom What're you getting at?

Truscott I am getting at the heart of this extremely distressing case, aren't I now?

Tom The heart ...?

Truscott (*rising*) Later, some years later, a person pleading guilty, I left court early, and, as an unremembered robber started on his ten years of close confinement, I began my sentence of suspicion.

Tom Sometimes, my dear Fennimore, you talk like a bad detective novel.

Truscott turns and looks at the conservatory and takes a step or two towards it

Truscott I crossed the lawn and stood facing the conservatory. I heard that damned perky little tune you still indulge in.

Tom (*singing quietly*) "*Che gelida manina,*
                              Se la lasci riscaldar.
                              Cercar che giova?
                              Al buio non si trova ..."

Truscott The windows of the conservatory were misted. I saw nothing but shapes.

Tom (*singing*)   "*Ma per fortuna*
                              È una notta di luna,
                              E qui la luna
                              L'abbiamo vicina ..."

Truscott What were the two shadows on the greenish glass? A woman and a watering can merely, or two creatures of the opposite sex, unlawfully intermingled? I stood watching a long time. Then I scrunched my foot on the gravel to give you a fair warning. (*He moves back towards his chair*) But when I opened the conservatory door ——

Tom What did you see?

Truscott (*sitting*) My much-troubled wife.

Tom And ... ?

Truscott No one else.

Tom There now! Nothing to worry about.

Truscott The bird had flown.

Tom I was never there.

Truscott You'd fled. A very clear indication of guilt.

Tom If I hadn't been there, I couldn't have fled.

Truscott If you hadn't been there you couldn't've been whistling that damned tune!

Tom Perhaps Maggie whistled it.

Truscott My wife would never do such a thing. She's not musical. So far as I know.

Tom You may not know very far. Your wife is particularly addicted to the operas of Giacomo Puccini.

Truscott She never listens to music.

Tom She never listens, Fen, because she is afraid music would arouse in her romantic longings which you are quite unable to fulfil.

Truscott So, do you — ?

Tom What?

Truscott You, Marshbanks, do you fulfil them?

Tom What is the question, exactly?

Truscott (*to himself*) The question is, Members of the Jury, have you rogered my wife? (*Aloud*) Have you rogered her?

There is a pause

Tom Hadn't you better ask *her* that?

Truscott It's not the sort of question one asks a lady, is it?

Tom Anyway, why bring it up today — after all these years?

Truscott Isn't this just the day to bring it up? Edwin's coming to lunch.

Tom I see. Oh, I do see. (*He laughs*) Oh dear ... Oh deary me. Brass-rubbings! And water-colours!

Truscott (*voice of doom*) Yes?

Tom Poor old Fen! You didn't care for the idea of Edwin writing to me about — brass-rubbings!

Truscott I must confess, I found the evidence disturbing.

Tom You didn't care for it at all!

Truscott (*to himself*) It comes from an unreliable source, that is to say the mouth of the accused, but it is — disturbing evidence, all the same.

Tom What are you afraid of, Fennimore? That I'll take your immortality off you?

Truscott What are you talking about?

Tom Your claim on the years to come. A line of Truscotts, stretching out to the future. Passing judgement. Condemning! Locking people up! Endlessly censorious. Endlessly frightened of what their wives may be getting up to in the conservatory. The Truscotts of Gallows Corner!

Truscott Rather a better stock, wouldn't you say, than the Marshbanks of Craft Cottage, the potters of Folkweave Farm, the old fellows with moist blue eyes and spotted bow ties — you know, the ones whose war effort was whistling and keeping chickens. That line is coming to an abrupt end with you, Marshbanks! There will be no fruit of the loins you keep concealed in those filthy old corduroy bags!

Tom Is that your considered opinion?

Truscott What?

Tom Is that your final judgement on the matter?

Truscott Is there anything more you would wish to say?

There is silence

Mute of malice, are you?

Tom Is there anything more you would wish me to say?

Truscott I'm not fishing for information.

Tom Oh yes you are! You boast you're such a tough nut to crack but you're frightened. Admit it, Fennimore. Scared to death of what you might discover.

Truscott Scared? Scared of what?

Tom Edwin.

Truscott My son.

Tom Your son. With artistic leanings. Your son, who wrote to me regularly from Lawnhurst. Your son who's kept quiet all these years, doing what exactly? Throwing pots, perhaps. Using his fingers, light on the clay, a touch like velvet, to achieve a perfect symmetry! Is he really your son, do you think?

There is a pause

Truscott (*furiously*) Have you the slightest evidence to support that monstrous allegation?

Tom Only the evidence of your eyes. Take a good look at lunchtime, on your idea of the future.

Truscott Don't be ridiculous. I've looked at Edwin. I've seen the boy tearing round this very garden. I've bowled leg breaks to him down there on the edge of the paddock. At times — many times — I have felt bound to punish him and I must say he has respected me for it. The matter is proved beyond reasonable doubt. All doubt is fanciful. The lad is every inch a Truscott.

Tom If you think so.

Truscott What?

Tom I said ...

Truscott I heard what you said. I'm not deaf. What sort of answer is that — "If you think so"?

Tom It's not meant to be an answer, more a comment.

Truscott Not evidence. Pure comment.

Tom On your enormous complacency.

Truscott My ... ?

Tom You're so sure of everything, aren't you, Fennimore? I have sat in this garden now, ever since you moved to Gallows

Corner, or at your dinner table or at lunch, and I have been deafened by your appalling lack of doubt on every subject. Capital punishment. Corporal punishment. How to make marmalade. Everything appears perfectly simple to you, doesn't it? God is simply a senior Judge in the Court of Appeal. Death is merely a promotion to immortality. Geraniums are perfectly simple to manage if you don't mollycoddle them. And I — your next-door-neighbour — I have to stand in, now they've retired you at long, long last, for all those unfortunate criminals you miss so badly. I might refuse to visit you again. I'm tired of standing in the dock at Gallows Corner.

Truscott Never visit us — and not see Margaret?

Tom And not see either of you. It's been a life's work, keeping you both amused.

Truscott Do you suppose I find you amusing?

Tom Oh, of course, my pots. My bow ties. My alleged loose living. They keep you constantly entertained, don't they? And the fact that Maggie and I possibly had ... a relationship ——

Truscott Relationship? What sort of mealy-mouthed expression is that? Is that the word nice girls in smocks who hand-paint egg-cups use, when they rut? Why don't you say "roger" like everyone else?

Tom Because you're the only person I've ever heard say it.

There is a pause. Truscott stands

Truscott Have you rogered her? That is the question I have long had before me.

Tom Well, have you come to a final judgement?

Truscott Oh yes.

Tom And the verdict is "guilty", I suppose. It usually is.

Truscott I have directed myself as to reasonable doubt. Doubt is, in most cases, a form of cowardice. And now I have the painful duty of passing sentence.

Tom Why painful? Passing judgement's as natural to you as passing water.

Truscott In a shifting world, Marshbanks, in a bog of unreliable evidence, there is usually one hard fact, one stepping-stone of undisputed truth. And that is — I am Edwin's father!

Tom The complacency — of your legal decisions!

Truscott Whatever you may or may not have done — and I make no finding as to your activities save that they were furtive, devious and no doubt deeply embarrassing to the lady upon whom you inflicted your intentions — the paternity of Edwin is beyond dispute. How could it be otherwise?

Tom I thought you had an idea how it might be.

There is a pause. Truscott sits

Truscott (*smiling*) The idea is laughable. As you pass through life, Marshbanks, you may have noticed, you make very little impression on the universe. I can scarcely hear your step on the gravel. As you cross the lawn I never see footprints, even when the grass is frosted. You are a drop in the ocean, Marshbanks, a puff in the wind.

Tom So what are you worrying about?

Truscott I'm not worrying in the least. When I look at Edwin I have no doubts. No doubts whatever.

Tom It's a good many years since you looked at him.

Truscott When I look at Edwin I feel I have every reason to be proud of *my* boy.

Tom It takes very little, you know.

Truscott What?

Tom One small spermatozoon. All the rest, the thousands of wasted organisms might be described, this is as I understand it, as part of nature's bombast, her taste for wild exaggeration.

Truscott Do you wish to open the possibility?

Tom Not a possibility, my Lord. To me it is a certainty.

Truscott What?

Tom Why do you think I'm here for lunch?

Truscott To down my sherry, of course. To hack away at my vintage claret and gobble my duck. "Second-helping Marshbanks", that's what Margaret and I call you, behind your back, of course. (*He laughs*) "Second-helping."

Tom I came here to see you.

Truscott *My* boy. I don't follow ——

Tom Come off it, Fen. Could *you* produce a boy that knelt on a church floor, carefully tracing the shapes of dead crusaders, or who sat at an easel on a summer evening, painting the reflections in a reservoir? Could the fruit of *your* old legal loins write poetry, or stand beside me at the kiln and, when the shapes emerged in their perfection, stare breathless at the simplicity of art?

Truscott You had *my* Edwin with you, when you were cooking up chamber-pots?

Tom Oh, often on his holidays my Edwin came over. He would stay for tea and his mother would join us and we all played *Bohème*. I had Caruso, on the old seventy-eights.

Truscott Where was I?

Tom Hard at work, I imagine, imprisoning people.

Truscott (*bringing his hand down on the arm of his chair*) I cannot possibly accept this so-called evidence.

Tom Your wife was there when Edwin spun the wheel and made a little mug to take back to school with him. "Look at the boy's hands," she'd say. "He has long artistic fingers, like his father." Don't look at your hands, Fennimore. Short, stubby fingers, yours, fit for pointing out stab wounds on police photographs.

There is a pause

Truscott For the moment, I suggest we say nothing that would embarrass Margaret.

Tom Embarrass her?
Truscott As for you, Marshbanks——
Tom Prisoner at the Bar.
Truscott I shall deal with you later.

Margaret and another figure — male — appear in the conservatory

Margaret (*calling*) Boys!
Truscott (*turning and looking through the glass of the conservatory*) Is that Margaret?
Tom (*turning to look*) Of course it's Margaret.
Truscott Who's that with her? In the conservatory? Can't you see someone? Some shape.

Margaret comes out of the conservatory. We can see the other figure standing in the shadows of the conservatory behind her

Margaret (*to the figure*) They're sitting there gossiping. Nineteen to the dozen. Under the old mulberry tree. Heaven knows how they find so much to talk about. (*To the two men*) Edwin's here!
Truscott (*rising in greeting, looking towards the conservatory*) My son.
Tom (*rising*) My boy — young Edwin!
Truscott Well, there you are, Edwin. How are you, my boy?

CURTAIN

Scene 2

The same. Four o'clock in the afternoon

Truscott is in his chair, smoking a cigar. Tom is sitting also. The sherry decanter and the tray with glasses have gone

Truscott Edwin's gone.

Tom Oh, yes. The "limo" came for him.

Truscott The *what*?

Tom The limousine. Back to Global House.

Truscott Yes. Edwin's gone.

Tom Straight back to London. It seems he's "got a meeting".

Truscott Which is "top priority."

Tom And which he can't afford to miss. "Time's money," says Edwin.

Truscott Don't you agree?

Tom Not money any longer. Time seems to be our dwindling ability to stay alive.

There is a pause

Truscott Well, at long last, and after all these years, Edwin has been to luncheon! An opportunity to get to know the boy.

Tom Not much of an opportunity.

Truscott Oh, I don't need long, to get to know the ins and outs of a fellow. In my line of business one gets used to sizing up a witness, fairly quickly. One forms an impression.

Tom Of course, he's been a long time in Canada. You must make every allowance for that ...

Truscott It was good to see the boy again.

Tom And he didn't make much of an inroad on your sherry.

Truscott (*thoughtfully*) You noticed that? I noticed it also.

Tom I think we all noticed.

Truscott (*disappointed*) He rejected the Amontillado.

Tom He asked if we had any "juice."

Truscott You noticed that too, did you?

Tom "Is there a package of juice," he said, "in the ice box?"

Truscott I was not perfectly clear what the boy was driving at.

Tom Margaret told him. She told him that the milkman does "Dayglow Orange Drink" but we hadn't any.

Truscott I told him that the Amontillado was juice — juice of the grape cunningly qualified, but he was having none of it. (*He pauses*) And none of the claret at luncheon, either.

Tom It seems that Edwin has seen too many people with "alcohol-related problems". Among the "young executives in middle management".

Truscott I used to give Edwin wine for every birthday. On his tenth, as I remember it, I gave him four dozen of the Pichon Longueville. (*He pauses*) For laying down, not immediate consumption.

Tom Immediate drinking, at the age of ten?

Truscott When he was eleven I laid down five cases of the Cantenac Beychevelle for Edwin.

Tom We've made a few inroads on the cellar since then.

Truscott Not too many inroads. We've saved a great deal for the boy. (*He pauses*) Now it seems we've saved it for ourselves. (*He pauses*) He hardly touched his roast duck, did you notice also? Edwin hardly pecked at a drumstick.

Tom Cholesterol. He said he'd seen too much of that in business.

Truscott That was the reason he gave for doing such poor justice to the loganberry pie, and giving the cold shoulder to our cream boat.

Tom He said he'd seen too many young executives go through the same thing.

Truscott Loganberry pie?

Tom Open heart surgery.

Truscott Well, really. I've tackled loganberry pie regularly, man and boy, for a good many years.

Tom And your heart has remained as closed as ever.

Truscott Well, I've never been scared of a carving of duck. Let's put it that way, shall we?

Tom Of course, Edwin had a good breakfast. He told us that he will always start the day with a dish of breakfast cereal. Don't you remember Edwin telling us that, Fennimore?

Truscott Cereal! Is that those small segments of baked cardboard that come in packets? Cereal, it seems, is something Edwin's taken to since he's been away from us.

Tom Of course, he explained he doesn't really have time for anything else in the mornings. He's always "in a heck of a hurry getting to Global Computers."

Truscott "The Company."

Tom (*laughing*) He hasn't been doing much log-cabinning, has he? Not much running wild, as you suggested. He's spent ten years in the Global office in Toronto, rising to the executive floor by "the sheer damned will to succeed."

Truscott And I tell you something else! Edwin had absolutely no recollection of ever having rubbed a single brass. Not even when he was of tender years. He simply gave no support to your evidence of "artistic leanings". (*He pauses*) It also seems that he never wrote poetry on the subject of the wind.

Tom (*singing*)"*Che gelida manina,*
            Se la lasci riscaldar.
            Cercar che giova ..."

Truscott And he couldn't even remember you playing that damned ditty on your wind-up gramophone!

Tom Odd that he couldn't remember you bowling leg breaks to him either, down on the edge of the paddock. He never seems to have hit a six into the apple trees — and he couldn't remember a single one of your notable murders.

Truscott I asked him what he *did* remember. Well, in all fairness I thought I was bound to put the question.

Tom He remembered lying on his bed all the afternoon doing algebra.

Truscott He said the three of us were always talking together. He preferred his maths, it seems, to our company. (*He pauses*) Of course, I noticed that as a boy Edwin was not always with us. I thought he was behind the shrubbery somewhere, playing pirates.

Tom In fact he was doing sums!

Truscott Training himself for his professional life.

Tom His intimate knowledge of computers.

Truscott Didn't it occur to you that Edwin had a somewhat exaggerated respect for those no doubt useful little gadgets?

Tom He told you the law needed one of his "Global" machines. Put in all the facts and get the appropriate sentence out, that's what Edwin told you. Perhaps he's discovered how to dispense with Judges.

Truscott No doubt a computer could manufacture your peasant-style jerries without too much of an effort, Marshbanks. Perhaps you're due to be phased out completely.

Tom "Your sentences," said Edwin, "were influenced by the amount of port you drank the night before, or whether you'd quarrelled with Mother, or if Haversack had peed on the carpet." They could have replaced you years ago, Fennimore, with a decent calculating machine!

There is a pause

Margaret appears in the conservatory

Tom looks towards the conservatory and sees Margaret

Here comes Margaret.

Truscott (*looking at the conservatory*) Of course, you're very quick to spot her!

Margaret comes out of the conservatory

Margaret Edwin's gone.

Tom Yes.

Truscott It's a bit rum, isn't it, his not coming to see us for all those years.

Margaret Oh, he came to see us——

Tom What?

Margaret He came to England quite often in the autumn. But that's the time you used to like to go to Dieppe. You both used to like it there, in the autumn.

Tom So we missed Edwin!

Margaret Yes, we missed him. (*She sits in one of the chairs*)

Tom I suppose you could say it was our fault, really.

Truscott Well, you can't go to Dieppe in August. Gives you sun stroke. (*He pauses*) So we missed Edwin.

Margaret Well, yes.

Truscott And now he's gone.

Margaret He was talking to me just now. He dried up for me. In the kitchen.

Tom Before the "limo" came for him?

Margaret Yes. He was very helpful in that way. He dried up.

Truscott Handle a deft tea towel, does Edwin?

Margaret And he was saying that he'd avoided marriage for a good many years.

Tom He told us that at lunch. He said he'd seen too many "young executives" with marriage problems. It affected them, he told us. Just when they should be "maximizing their input for the company." "Marriage," Edwin thinks, "is one of the chief reasons for divorce."

Truscott It also leads to crime, that's been my experience after a good many years on the Bench.

Margaret Well, Edwin seems to have high hopes for his marriage with Arlene.

Truscott Whoever's Arlene?

Margaret Arlene Jackson. Daughter of the Vice President in charge of Media Promotion ...

Tom He never told *us* about Arlene.

Truscott Perhaps he thought it was something more suitable for his mother to deal with.

Margaret And of course they're getting this house together.

Truscott Who are?

Margaret Edwin and Arlene.

Truscott They'll need one if they're getting married. I don't know what you'd have done without *our* matrimonial home, Marshbanks. You'd have been hard put to it to know where to turn for a free luncheon!

Margaret It seems Edwin's being put in charge of the California office. They've got a big house on the beach. Edwin says life's very easy there. The marketing's so simple.

Truscott Marketing?

Margaret You just drive in and park behind the supermarket and someone will carry it out for you. And it's never cold. The weather's the same every day on the coast, except for a little fog occasionally. (*He pauses*) He thinks this place is too big for us. The garden's too much to keep up, Edwin thinks, and Cattermole's getting too old to cope with it. And one other thing ——

Truscott What other thing?

Margaret He thinks you quarrel too much.

Truscott Quarrel?

Margaret You and Tom quarrel. Edwin says it's not a happy atmosphere. He's worried about me, as his mother.

Truscott Well, of course we quarrel.

Tom Isn't that what neighbours are for?

Margaret Edwin finds it strange that you quarrel so much, and then go on holiday together.

Truscott So does Edwin offer any solution — to this allegedly puzzling situation?

Margaret Edwin recommends a change.

Tom For all of us?

Margaret It would amount to that. Edwin wanted me to tell you his idea. He thought that might be better.

Truscott Edwin has an idea, has he? A "wheeze". Is it something brilliant?

Margaret Of course, it would mean putting Gallows Corner on the market.

Truscott Gallows Corner to be sold? (*He pauses*) Less than brilliant.

Margaret What Edwin said was: he felt he had to get nearer to us. That was it! He wanted to come much closer.

Truscott Aren't we too old for that?

Tom He said all this during the washing up?

Margaret He feels that he owes it to us to look after us in our old age. He wanted you to consider it carefully.

Truscott Consider what, exactly?

Margaret Edwin says there's plenty of room in their new house on the coast.

Truscott Plenty of room for what?

Margaret For his father, and mother of course.

Truscott The coast of *what* was it again?

Margaret The coast of America. Edwin wants his father to live there too.

Tom And Arlene.

Margaret And Arlene, of course.

There is a pause

Truscott He distinctly said he wanted his "father" to join the happy couple on the coast? That is your clear recollection?

Margaret I promised I'd ask you to think about it.

Truscott Well, doesn't that pose rather a question?

Margaret Yes.

Truscott You know, Marshbanks. I have been thinking about young Edwin since he left us this afternoon.

Margaret It's getting cold in the garden. Shouldn't we be going indoors?

Truscott Edwin wishes his father to join him on "the coast". Is that the simple point at issue, Margaret?

Margaret Yes. (*She gets up*) I'm going indoors to put the kettle on. We'll have to light a log fire this evening. (*She moves towards the conservatory*) Why don't you come in? You've both sat out past any sensible time for sitting.

Truscott Presently, Margaret. We'll be in for tea presently.

Margaret goes into the house, through the conservatory

Tom Edwin'll look after you in America, Fennimore. He'll probably put you on a diet. Just juice and wheatgerm!

Truscott However serious the situation, Marshbanks, you can be relied on to say something entirely trivial. What do you call that — artistic licence?

Tom Oh, you'll lose weight on the coast, won't you? You'll leave your stomach in San Francisco ——

Truscott Do you never glance in the mirror? It's your figure that shows every sign of a lifetime's self-indulgence ... of the grossest sort.

Tom Steady on, old fellow. No need to get personal.

Truscott I don't care for that "old fellow". Coming from you, "old fellow" grates.

There is a pause

Tom (*smiling*) Of course, life in California may change you, Fennimore.

Truscott Change me?

Tom All that lying in the sun. And going barefoot along the beach. Do you think you might become a beachcomber, Fennimore? Wear "sneakers" and give up shaving?

Truscott Oh, Marshbanks. Do be very careful.

Tom Or take up some ... musical instrument. The guitar perhaps. (*He is hardly able to stop himself laughing during the following*) Shall we possibly see you on summer nights on the porch, strumming the guitar — and tricked out in beads?

Truscott There is such a thing as Contempt of Court, you know. Deliberate Contempt, in the face of the tribunal.

Tom (*standing*) I'm going in to tea. (*He pauses*) I forget ... am I still on trial? (*He moves away*)

Truscott Still very much on trial. And you would do well to remember it.

Tom exits

There is a pause

Margaret (*off; calling*) Are you coming, Fen?

Margaret enters from the conservatory

You're missing your tea.

There is a pause

Sitting out here any longer you'll miss your tea entirely.

Truscott What a tragedy!

Margaret Not a tragedy, Fen. But a pity. Perhaps.

Truscott There are certain things more important than tea. You wouldn't understand that, of course.

Margaret I suppose there are. But not many things, I should have thought. Not for us, nowadays. (*She sits in the chair nearest to Truscott*)

Truscott There are certain things vastly more important.

Margaret Oh, I suppose you mean your little trials.

Truscott My "little" trials, as you are pleased to call them, are a means to an end. And that end is the truth. Now, as ever, the truth of the matter is vital! Absolutely vital!

Margaret Well, you won't find it out with a trial, will you?

Truscott A trial in a British court, Margaret, is the one sure way of arriving at the facts.

Margaret (*smiling*) Do you really believe that? All that dressing up. And wigs. And long speeches. And people swearing on bibles. And tripping each other up with silly questions. Do you really think that ever solves anything?

Truscott (*grumbling*) All these long years I've been married to an anarchist.

Margaret All it proves is that men like putting on a performance. I've always thought it's got about as much to do with telling the truth as amateur theatricals.

Truscott (*shocked*) Amateur theatricals?

Margaret I'm sorry, Fen. I didn't mean to hurt your feelings.

Truscott You're speaking of matters you're quite unqualified to understand.

Margaret Oh, dear, yes. I suppose I am.

Truscott Can you or any member of the Red persuasion think of a better method of finding out exactly what happened?

There is a pause

Margaret Please don't ask me, Fen.

Truscott Of course you can't!

Margaret You really shouldn't ask me! (*She stands*) It's not for me to tell you. (*She pauses, looking down at him*) Anyway. There is one thing.

Truscott What?

Margaret When you were in court it never stopped you having your tea. I remember your clerk made Earl Grey in the Judge's room. In the bone china.

Truscott Leave me a moment, Margaret. I have matters to consider.

Margaret You're not coming in?

Truscott Not yet. No.

Margaret (*moving away*) Well, of course you must please yourself entirely.

Margaret exits into the conservatory; during the following she is joined by Tom

Truscott (*speaking to the audience as though they are a jury*) Members of the Jury. On the evidence you have heard, you may have no doubt that the prosecution have made out an over-whelming case. I believe there is no alternative to a verdict of guilty on the first count of the indictment. The charge of the unlawful rogering of Lady Margaret Truscott by the man Marshbanks has been proved entirely to my satisfaction. I only wish I could say, "That is the end of the matter" and discharge you from further deliberation. But one vital issue still remains. Did that unlawful act cause the birth of a male child, known to posterity as Edwin Truscott? (*He turns to look at the conservatory*)

The figures of Tom and Margaret can be seen through the greenish glass. We hear the small sound of their laughter

It is rare, Members of the Jury, for us to be able to observe, during the course of a trial, the accused and his accomplice at the scene of a crime. I would urge you to take full advantage of that opportunity. Watch carefully. Are they talking in an animated manner? You might have thought that at their age,

and after so long an acquaintance, they would have run out of
ordinary innocent conversation. You might have expected the
two of them to have fallen into a decent silence. If they have not,
does it argue a *tête-à-tête* of a most intimate nature? Could they
possibly be discussing Edwin's invitation to join him in the
United States of America? Members of the Jury, the issue of
parentage is always a painful one, but painful issues must be
faced. At this stage of the trial you will not flinch or fail. You
will soldier on. (*He sits on for a moment and then rises slowly
and walks towards the conservatory*)

*The Lights fade to indicate a passage of time and come up again
quickly. The stage is empty. Truscott and Tom come out into the
garden, closing the conservatory door behind them*

Tom I will say this for old Maggie. She puts on a rattling good
tea.

Truscott (*sitting and talking judicially*) I am reminded of a
number of different pieces of evidence, unimportant in them-
selves perhaps, but fitted together they add up to an unanswer-
able case.

Tom Oh dear. Are we to have another case?

Truscott A short one only. And one of which the result may be
not unwelcome to you.

Tom You mean I'm not to be condemned to death.

Truscott Eventually, of course. But not, perhaps, today.

Tom Well, Fen, let's hear it.

Truscott I would start by reminding you ... (*To himself*) I am sure
you will remember the evidence, Members of the Jury, with the
attention you have clearly been paying throughout this unfortunate case... (*Aloud*) Edwin takes breakfast cereal.

Tom *Your* Edwin.

Truscott Edwin, I repeat, ingests some pre-packaged prepara-
tion on rising. He is also, as it has been admitted, an addict of

"juice". When faced with a duck drumstick he babbles of cholesterol, when offered a healthy glass of claret, which can only have the effect of raising the spirits and keeping the bowels regular, he is visited by dark thoughts of alcoholism and loss of employment. How would you describe a fellow, Marshbanks, who puts off marriage, as you have put it off?

Tom Sensible.

Truscott "Sensible" or ... (*with disgust*) would you say "artistic"? A vegetarian, an addict of free love — and knickerbockers. Just the sort to indulge himself in brass-rubbings, and water-colours, if you want my opinion. A pale and unhealthy youth, if I may charge my recollection, who when other lads were playing pirates in the orchard, lay up on his bed doing quadratic equations.

Tom (*puzzled*) Other lads?

Truscott An underminer of married life, witness his determined attempt to "sell up" Gallows Corner.

Tom Not a sound scheme, that, of Edwin's.

Truscott Almost as bad, would you say, as haunting conservatories when a husband's back is turned, as creeping around with a handful of eggs, whistling tender moments from the repertoire of Italian caterwaulers? Edwin is a chip off the old block, if you ask my opinion.

Tom A — what?

Truscott Like father, like son! Blood may be thicker than water, even though, in the case of the Marshbanks family, it emerges in the form of "juice".

Tom *My* family?

Truscott Oh, chuck it, Tom. It's clear as mud. He couldn't be mine! Edwin is *your* boy!

Tom My ... ?

Truscott Your son! The fruit of your loins. I suppose, given the somewhat spare and skinny nature of the loins in question, the fruit is as sour and meagre as might be expected.

Tom My son? Now look here, Fennimore ——

Truscott Your by-blow! Your little bit of the wrong side of the blanket. A potter's bastard, spawned from a quick clutch in the conservatory, a hasty embrace behind the aspidistras. If anyone has to go and live on "the coast" it should certainly be you!

Tom I begin to see what's happening. A miscarriage of justice! No, *you* go, Fennimore. He's your responsibility!

Truscott As you hinted, Edwin is a sensitive plant. Takes after his father. Of course he wrote to you from Lawnhurst. What did you send your sprig, Marshbanks, a hot water bottle and a couple of chest protectors?

Tom Edwin, if you want my opinion, has not got the soul of an artist.

Truscott But he's got the artist's infallible instinct for winkling respectable people out of their homes.

Tom What artist has ever been known to lie on his bed doing quadratic equations?

Truscott Suppose you tell me. Wasn't the poet Shelley a bit of a one for the higher mathematics?

Tom The poet Shelley, you can take it from me, Fennimore, had never even heard of algebra.

Truscott You're sure?

Tom The main characteristic of young Edwin ——

Truscott Not so young.

Tom — of Edwin, I would say, is his grasp of business matters, his lack of imagination, the plodding, not to say pedantic manner in which he expresses himself. In any conceivable cricket team of crashing bores, *your* Edwin would undoubtedly be first in to bat.

Truscott *My* Edwin? Oh, do be very careful, Marshbanks. Did you say *my* Edwin, by any chance?

Tom With a bore of that magnitude, there's bound to be a lawyer in his pedigree. Besides, Edwin could never be anything as interesting as a bastard. That young man was conceived with the utmost respectability, one night, perhaps, when you had become overexcited by a day imposing deterrent sentences and Maggie closed her eyes and hummed Puccini to herself.

Truscott Oh, be careful!

Tom What will you get me for? Contempt of Court?

Truscott Could I have given birth to a boy who rejected the Pichon Longueville?

Tom Oh, easily. You believe in character-building, don't you? In self-discipline. Free will and taking the tough decision. Well, your boy has just disciplined himself out of a decent wine. Anyway, he looks just like you.

Truscott Like me! Put him up to the light and you could see through him.

Tom Before you grew that stomach and your nose went purple, he's the spitting image.

Truscott Of you, Marshbanks. Put a spotted bow tie round the boy's neck and he'd look every inch a potter!

Tom A lawyer, Fennimore. Every inch a lawyer.

Truscott Nonsense!

Tom A development, of course, since your vintage. Edwin is "le Truscott nouveau", a fresh and impertinent young wine with a greatly increased boring factor.

Truscott Not a Truscott! "Nouveau" or anything else. (*He gets up and moves to look at the garden*)

Tom (*rising and following Truscott*) Edwin is your gift to the future, Fennimore. The man who makes his decisions with a machine, with no small error of mercy possible.

Truscott He's a bloody vegetarian brass-rubber.

Tom Rubbish. Anyway, *I'm* not a vegetarian!

Truscott You're a duck-gobbling, poultry-eating vegetarian!

Tom There is only one thing to be said of Edwin. He is clearly not my responsibility!

During the following speech Margaret appears behind the conservatory windows with another — male — figure

Truscott Nothing's your responsibility, is it? That's what's wrong with you, Marshbanks. I've heard it a thousand times. "I don't know what made me do it, my Lord." You know quite well what made you do it. A taste for rogering married ladies! And now you must simply face up to the appalling consequences of your actions!

There is a pause

Tom (*looking at the conservatory*) Is that Maggie ... up there in the conservatory?

Truscott A brief spasm of so-called delight, and a lifetime of Edwin to look forward to. Given his ridiculous anxiety to remain alive he'll probably reach ninety.

Tom Is there someone up there in the conservatory, with Maggie?

Truscott (*looking towards the conservatory*) Probably Edwin.

Tom Edwin left to go back to London.

Truscott She must be alone then. It's the shape, the shadows on that green glass that are confusing.

Margaret comes out of the conservatory and moves towards the two men

Margaret Still out there chattering! Whatever do you two find to talk about?

Truscott Something about which we would like your honest ... opinion. Sit down for a moment. (*He sits*) Please, make yourself comfortable, madam.

Tom (*warningly*) Fennimore! (*He sits*)

Truscott It's no go, Marshbanks. We can't live forever in a state of suspended speculation. The time has come when a decision has to be reached, however painful.

Margaret What is it now? Has Haversack been digging in the flowerbeds again?

Tom No, Maggie. It's not Haversack.

Truscott I'm afraid the issues raised here are rather more serious.

Margaret More serious than Haversack digging in the new rose bed? There's a last little splash of sunshine. I will sit with you, just for a few moments. (*She sits*)

Truscott I will now call Lady Margaret Truscott.

Margaret I'm here, Fennimore. You don't need to call me.

Truscott I had hoped to deal with this matter without troubling you to give evidence, without you having to recall facts of a no doubt painful and embarrassing nature.

Margaret And for supper, I thought cold cuts, on a tray in front of the fire.

Truscott Madam. The allegations that have been brought against me personally are of such a grave nature that the matter must be cleared up now, before any adjournment is granted.

Margaret I know no law. I really can't join in your game. Shan't we all go in?

Truscott Until my name is cleared, we do not go in!

Margaret What is it, Tom? Can you understand him?

Tom Oh yes, Maggie. I can understand.

Truscott I leave aside the questionable behaviour of this man Marshbanks. I pass no judgement on whether or not and in what precise circumstances you were rogered by him.

Margaret (*sighing*) Oh, Fen dear. Not that again.

Truscott The present position is far more serious. The charge is that I fathered the person Edwin. That I, Sir Fennimore Truscott, Q.C., one of Her Majesty's Judges of the Queen's Bench, retired and put out to grass, did maliciously burden the future with the said person, thereby diminishing, to that extent, the quality of life on earth.

Tom Tell him, Maggie. Who was Edwin's father?

Margaret Do you wish it were you?

Tom No. Quite honestly.

Margaret Neither of you wants him. (*She pauses; then stands*) Come on, boys. Let's go indoors.

Truscott Not until you have answered my question.

Margaret How can I make you understand?

Truscott I propose to call Lady Margaret Truscott. I assume the witness wishes to affirm.

Margaret Affirm what?

Truscott Being of the Red persuasion she wishes to swear to the truth in some mealy-mouthed secular fashion.

Margaret I don't know why I should have the responsibility——

Tom What we want to know quite simply, Maggie, is *which* of us?

Truscott Which of us is responsible for what I suppose might be called the "younger generation" who may or may not, in the course of time, inherit our bits and pieces. (*He pauses*) To me, Edwin has the distinct smell of a Marshbanks to him.

Tom To me he is all Truscott.

Margaret (*moving away to look at the garden*) Edwin. My son.

Truscott On that issue there can be no room for doubt, I imagine.

Tom No doubt he wants you to go out there, Maggie?

Margaret He meant it well, I'm sure, when he invited me.

Tom What did you say? I mean, what were your feelings, exactly?

Margaret Oh, I told him I couldn't go. I had to get the geraniums in. On the coast, it seems, the geraniums may stay out all of the year round. "Well," I said, "that doesn't leave much for a gardener to do."

Tom What did Edwin say to that?

Margaret "Geraniums," he told me, "are not everything. The future is out there on the coast," he said. Quite honestly, Edwin can't find the future here.

Tom Can he not? What have you done with the future, Fen?

Truscott You're not going with him, are you, Margaret?

There is a pause

Margaret If I thought of it — I'd have to talk the matter over with Edwin's father.

Tom But you've done that, Maggie!

Margaret No. I don't think I could. It would cause embarrassment. I'm not sure his wife would like it.

Tom His wife?

Truscott I'm not quite catching the drift of this evidence ...

Margaret (*moving back towards the men*) Edwin talks about the future. Well, I certainly wasn't thinking about the future — not that summer before the year when Edwin was born.

Tom A good summer, as I remember, particularly in the soft fruit department.

Margaret Every day starting with the sun melting the mist over the herbaceous border. It seems to me, looking back on it, a time of love ... (*She sits*)

Truscott Quite clearly of love, among other crimes.

Tom Go on ...

Margaret I loved you, Tom, because you were so strong and independent. Tough as old boots, caring about your pots and the rest of the world could go hang as far as you were concerned.

Truscott Tom? Strong? I can't say I follow the drift of this evidence.

Margaret And you, Fen, because of that ridiculous vulnerability ...

Truscott Perhaps, madam, you're not feeling quite yourself.

Margaret You cared so desperately about what people thought. You wanted to please everyone.

Truscott *Everyone!*

Margaret The police officers, and the jury. I used to see you in Court, trying to seduce the jury. I think you even tried to flatter the criminals by pretending their little crimes were so desperately important.

Tom (*laughing*) She's caught you neatly, Fen!

Truscott I hope we may be coming to a less frivolous part of the evidence ...

Margaret I mean, you may love someone, you may love the way they spin a potter's wheel with such outrageous confidence, or go to work at the Law Courts each morning trembling with fear and trying to put a ridiculously brave face on it. And you may love the way someone prunes roses, stooping so easily, or weeds the strawberry bed all day in the hot sunshine, with the dark stain of sweat growing on the back of his shirt.

Tom I'm lost. Do you prune roses, Fennimore?

Truscott Never. Neither do you. That's a job we always leave to Cattermole. Cattermole's the expert.

Tom Cattermole?

Margaret But just because you love someone, just because one summer... Well. I can't see that I'm responsible ...

Tom And wasn't it Cattermole who, more often than not, weeded the strawberry bed ... ?

Margaret Just because I may have laid myself down from time to time that summer ...

Truscott In the conservatory?

Margaret Oh, the orchard or the conservatory. I can't remember everything.

Truscott Oh try, madam. Do your best to charge your recollection.

Margaret What I mean is ...

Truscott Yes, madam. Tell us exactly what you do mean. So that we may note it down.

The second male figure appears in the conservatory, vaguely outlined against the glass

Margaret I mean, just because you fancy the way a man stands patiently picking out seed boxes, that doesn't make you responsible, does it, for the future?

Tom What are you trying to tell us, Maggie?

Margaret To tell you? (*She gives a small laugh*) Don't both look so solemn. (*She pauses*) How could we have run this great place without Cattermole to help us out? (*She pauses, getting up and moving towards the conservatory*) I'm going in now. Up to the house. I'm cold and I really can't tell you any more about it.

She exits into the conservatory, joining the figure behind the glass

Tom She's gone.
Truscott Up to the house?
Tom Into the conservatory?

They both look at the conservatory

Truscott Can you see her? We must get that glass cleaned occasionally. Now I can see her. I can see a shape.
Tom *One* shape, Fennimore. Is that all you can see?
Truscott Yes, I think so. I honestly think so.

The two figures behind the conservatory glass move away so that the conservatory looks empty

Truscott What was Margaret saying about our jobbing gardener, Cattermole? I'm not entirely sure I got the drift of her evidence.
Tom Are you not, Fennimore? Are you really not sure?
Truscott (*resigned*) Well, then. I suppose I am. (*He pauses*) The sun's dropped down behind the herbaceous border. Time to go in?
Tom Well, yes, I suppose it is.
Truscott (*standing*) You'll stay for supper, won't you, Marshbanks?
Tom (*getting up*) You really want me ... ?
Truscott (*laughing*) "Second-helping Marshbanks". The unfortunate fact is — I'm not sure we can do without you.

The two men move towards the conservatory together

Truscott One thing to be thankful for. Edwin has left us a bottle or two. Shall we have time, I wonder, to get through it all?

Tom Edwin! What do you think honestly? Is Edwin the future?

Truscott Not ours, Tom. Let's thank God for it. Not ours!

They exit into the conservatory and move into the house together

CURTAIN

FURNITURE AND PROPERTY LIST

On stage: Four basket chairs
Garden table
Panama hat

Off stage: Tray. *On it*: decanter of sherry and four sherry glasses (**Tom**)

Scene 2

Set: Cigar

Strike: Tray, decanter and glasses

LIGHTING PLOT

Property fittings required: nil

Exterior. The same throughout

To open: General exterior lighting

Cue 1   **Truscott** walks towards the conservatory (Page 33)
         Fade lights and bring up again quickly

Printed by John Good Holbrook